Behold the Man

A study of Jesus' humanity

Richard C George

The way of
THE SPIRIT

This booklet is based on one of a series of four talks given at Roffey Place in the summer of 2001. The lecture is contained in the CD that accompanies this booklet as part of the short course teaching material, and also as one part of a four-tape set entitled 'Jesus – Fully God and Fully Man'.

Copies are available from The Way of the Spirit.

2nd Edition published in Great Britain in 2007
by The Way of the Spirit, Unit 6, High Street, Loddon, Norfolk NR14 6AH
(01508) 520003
Registered Charity No. 1110648

Copyright © 2002 Richard C George

All rights reserved. No part of this publication may be reproduced, stored in a retrieval system, or transmitted, in any form or by any means, electronic, mechanical, photocopying, recording or otherwise, without the permission, in writing, of the publisher.

ISBN 1-900409-34-8
Scripture taken from the
HOLY BIBLE, NEW INTERNATIONAL VERSION.
Copyright © 1973, 1978, 1984 by
International Bible Society. Used by
permission of Hodder and Stoughton Limited.

How to Use This Booklet

It is arranged in two parts:
- The first (pages 10-22) introduces the theme of the humanity of Jesus from the pages of scripture.
- The second (pages 23-29) is a three-part study sheet made up of questions.

A single teaching CD with a talk to accompany the study guide is also available, as is the CD set 'Jesus - fully God, fully man' of which the CD accompanying this study is the same as CD number two. (To obtain this, please write to The Way of the Spirit.)

You can use this booklet in several different ways:

1. By itself with your Bible.
2. Along with the CD and your Bible.
3. By studying in a group.

Whichever method you adopt, learn to listen for what the Holy Spirit has to tell you—about your beliefs, attitudes and life-style. Ask yourself what lessons you should be learning from your readings, so that you can apply them to your own understanding and life as a Christian.

Part Two, the reading guide, has introductory notes on page 23 with further suggestions about how to use the study. Each part of this section has questions that will help you determine what you have learned and encourage you to apply that in practical living. The notes have been prepared in such a way that you can use them privately or in a group. Experience has shown that group study is much more fruitful.

If you use the CD, you may find it helpful to listen to the relevant part before starting your readings, but, if so, you should also listen to it again afterwards. Not all the answers to the questions will be found in the booklet—this is intentional!

If you use this booklet in a group you will need to listen to the CD early in your meeting. Then discuss your answers to the questions, share your insights and encourage one another to grow in the Lord. Remember to allow time for prayer and fellowship as well.

THE WAY OF THE SPIRIT
BIBLE READING COURSE

The purpose of this booklet and the CD that goes with it is partly to give you some impression of how *The Way of the Spirit Bible Reading Course* works. It is not, however, just an excerpt or collection of excerpts from the fuller course, but a properly integrated short course in its own right, and as such is somewhat different in presentation.

- The full course takes you systematically through the whole Bible chapter by chapter with the help of a proper textbook; here you have only a short booklet giving a brief survey of a Bible theme.
- The full course has more comprehensive worksheets.
- The course CD's offer more systematic teaching arranged in twenty-minute parts; the tape accompanying this booklet contains one continuous sermon.

Nevertheless, by using these materials you should capture the flavour of the full course quite well. The purpose of *The Way of the Spirit* is to teach about the livingness of the Bible and the power of the Spirit revealed in its pages, to help Christians understand what the Bible is all about, what the way of God's Spirit is in it, and how to enter more fully into the richness of life men and women of Bible-times enjoyed. You should find all these aims met in some measure as you follow *Behold the Man*.

If, after this short study, you wish to proceed to the fuller course, please write to us for further information, or visit our web site at **http://www.thewayofthespirit.com**

I dedicate this work to the fond memory
of John McKay, whose pioneering
ministry in the Word and Spirit transformed the
way I read the Bible and changed the
direction of my life.

Preface to the Second Edition

I will never forget the moment, sitting in John McKay's office, when I first truly appreciated that Jesus had been fully human. It wasn't that I'd not been intellectually aware of the fact, just that I'd never really seen it; I'd had no revelation.

I was part of a group studying the passage in Luke where Moses and Elijah joined Jesus on the mountain (I describe this scene later in this booklet) and I suddenly saw that the Jesus of the gospels really had been a man. I no longer heard the conversation around me, I was rapt. Just like the disciples at the end of the gospel, the Holy Spirit had opened my eyes and I now understood what I had read; my heart burned within me and I read the gospel accounts, particularly Luke, with new excitement, finding plentiful evidence of his manhood.

Studying at university later, I came to appreciate the full theological significance of the incarnation, that the one who was truly God had become truly man. Jesus: fully God yet fully man! On finishing that season of (at least in part!) deeply enriching academic theological study, and beginning to teach Bible college students, I discovered that many, like me, had an understanding of Jesus' humanity without really having revelation of it. I was eager to share what the bible taught and when I did, others' hearts seemed to burn too.

I was once challenged to explain why I thought this subject so important, when today Jesus is glorified and sitting at the right hand of God. Here's my now considered reply!

1. It seems to me that seeing that Jesus was fully human during his life on earth is a necessary step in appreciating his position today, which is seated at the right hand of his Father in heaven in his glorified resurrection body.

It's so easy for our delight in Jesus' deity to overwhelm the fact of his humanity – we can forget there is now a man in heaven, and the necessary prequel to his present position was his life, death and resurrection *as a man*. In other words, we relate to him more correctly (and therefore more gloriously and effectively) if we have come to terms with his bona fide humanity.

2. An African student at Roffey Place once shared with me how significant he felt this teaching was for his country, Kenya. He told me how many African Christian leaders are set up on a pedestal as if they were a necessary link between the congregation and God, and that congregations (knowing no better) have often allowed and even encouraged this. Once this student saw how genuinely human Jesus had been, he was free to see his leaders as fully human too. It is a great equaliser to know that God became a man; that no matter what gifting or anointing a man or woman may carry today we remain human. There is no place for any man or woman to stand between us and God; Jesus made the way for each of us to approach his throne directly.

The more the church engages (quite necessarily and appropriately) with the 'otherness' of God - that which we may call 'supernatural' - the more she could do with hanging on tightly also to Jesus' humanity – and her own too!

So, as we accept and delight in our own humanity so we don't fall into the trap of attempting to escape from it. Jesus was authentically human and that is what we are meant to be. Creation (including humanity) was good in the beginning (Genesis 1-2) and will be again (Isaiah 65.17-25 & Revelation 21). In touch with his manhood, we become less likely to escape into some sort of super-spiritual existence that is unrelated to what we are truly called and redeemed to be.

4. Any heightening of our understanding of what it cost God to redeem us will help us to pay the price of truly following him. For the creator to become a creature was an extraordinary and costly gesture.

5. Finally, to understand Jesus as a man who leant upon and relied on the Holy Spirit for his whole life (as is clear from the gospel accounts, especially Luke) is to understand that as we lean on the same Holy Spirit then we can indeed walk as Christ walked. His life is not out of

reach, he simply lived the normal human life – just as we now can. To see this is life-changing!

Of course we fail, yet every time we do, as we once *look again towards his holy temple* (Jonah 2.4), he picks us up and brings us back to that 'normal Christian life' he has for us: a life of obedience and dependence upon him which enables us to truly overcome all that might prevent us living the victorious life Christ intends for us.

It was sometime later, probably once I'd started training Prophetic Bible Teachers, that I re-read 'When the Veil is Taken Away[1]', and was encouraged to be reminded how central a concept Jesus' humanity is to the heart of The Way of the Spirit. In it John McKay uses the term 'shared experience' to describe how our experiences of God are essentially no different from the men and women of bible times: Ezekiel, Isaiah, Abraham, et al.

The foremost life we look to in this way, now that we understand he was genuinely human, is Jesus. The pattern for his life and ministry becomes the pattern for our charismatic careers; God encountered him as a man and we do too. In seeing Jesus this way he is lifted from an out-of-reach, highly spiritual, part-man, part-God figure to a more easily identifiable human figure *tempted in every way just as we are* (Hebrews 4.15b), who therefore can truly serve as a model for our human existence, our whole lives and our walks with God. Seeing this raises us to a place, for all the reasons mentioned above, where we can live out with confidence our call to be overcomers.

When I finished writing the first edition of 'Behold the Man', I was frustrated because I felt I wasn't expressing the fullness of what I had seen. Yet I have received many testimonies from people who have engaged with this bible study and have themselves been thrilled by what God has shown them. Of course it is in the study of the bible itself that people find life, and not in our words, so in line with all The Way of the Spirit material this booklet is intended to drive people to

---

[1] *When the Veil is Taken Away* by John McKay is available through The Way of the Spirit web shop.

the bible. It is not my opinion (or anybody else's) about Jesus' humanity that will change us, but revelation of it from the Holy Spirit!

So beware any who come to this expecting eloquent and illuminating ideas from man – my passionate wish is that you will be driven to the words of God in scripture and find the life of the Spirit of Christ therein.

Having received feedback following the publication of the first edition, I realised that two weeks was not enough to properly consider some of the questions raised, so one of the changes I have made in this second edition is to spread the questions over three weeks, adding one or two new ones.

Richard C George
Norwich, June 2007

PART ONE

Introduction

Since the children have flesh and blood, he too shared in their humanity...

(Hebrews 2:14)

A statue of Jesus stood in Trafalgar Square recently. It was sited on a large plinth in the shadow of the 165 foot tall Nelson's Column. The plinth was amongst other large plinths on which sat equally large lions. The whitened figure of Jesus, beardless and clad only in a loincloth and crown of thorns, was only six feet tall. Jesus looked small, insignificant and very human.

This statue, called 'Ecce Homo' ('Behold the man'), conveyed a great truth: that when Jesus Christ walked the face of this earth he did so as one who was fully human.

We all know that it takes an act of God to reveal Jesus' divinity to us; I was surprised to discover that it also takes an act of God to reveal his humanity. When I first saw, by revelation, that Jesus was truly human as well as divine it captivated me and brought my understanding of Jesus into line with what I now see is contained within the pages of scripture.

This study therefore is not concerned with Jesus' divinity, which I will take as read and which will be the subject of a later short course; I assume that each reader already has a revelation that Jesus is God. Nor am I concerned to venture into all the early church (or more modern) debates about the way in which Jesus may be thought of as being both fully man and fully God—there is a place for that but that place is not here. This short course will limit itself to the way in which scripture presents Jesus to us as a man, taking only an occasional sideways glance at his divinity.

Wrong Thinking!

How do you think of Jesus? Many Christians understand (maybe without having ever really had cause to think about it) that Jesus is man and God, yet somehow attribute different aspects of his life and ministry to whichever category seems more appropriate. E.g. on one hand he was able to work miracles, relate to his Father in heaven, or calm the wind and rain because he was divine, on the other hand, he wept with Mary at the news of the death of Lazarus or struggled in the garden of Gethsemane because he was human.

In other words, we imagine that Jesus of Nazareth was somehow part-man, part-God, the 'God' bit being the element that enabled him to perform miracles, and the man-bit there to feel sad or display other human qualities. Or, even worse, that he was actually God walking around on earth in appearance of a man; that somehow every appearance of humanity, e.g. struggling to carry out his heavenly Father's plan to go all the way to the cross, was somehow put on to give the impression that he was one of us, when all the time he was God 'in disguise'. These wrong views are perfectly understandable, after all we need to be able to, in some way, reconcile his manhood and divinity, and something along one of these lines is perhaps the simplest way to do it.

Unfortunately however, if we hold these views we end up with a 'mixed up' Jesus – one who is half God and half man - we end up watering down both. So let's lay aside his divinity (which may be a good enough way, at least for our purposes here, of understanding what he did with it!) and focus on Jesus the man.

Jesus the Word

In the beginning was the Word, and the Word was with God, and the Word was God ... the Word became flesh and made his dwelling among us...

(John 1:1,14)

The opening 14 verses of John's gospel are among some of the most exciting in the bible. They show us that the one called the 'Word', who was with God from 'the beginning', but who is also actually God, came himself into our world as flesh, that is, as a man. He became something which he was not and shared our creaturely weakness.

Having been with God in eternity—indeed he was the one through whom creation came into being (compare John 1:1 with Genesis 1:1-2; see also Colossians 1:16)—he became one of the creatures, sharing in our limitations and living as one of us.

That God became man shows us something of the eternal value and significance of human life to God. That he himself would choose to leave eternity, where he lacked nothing, and come and live as a creature within the earthly, temporal, sphere is nothing short of remarkable. Once we see what he did for us (even before the cross), it is hard not to respond by giving our all back to him. A true revelation of the incarnation (the technical term for God becoming man) also forces us to question how we relate to one another, deeply challenging the attitudes we hold towards our fellow creatures – if God values man that much, so must we!

Of all the gospel writers John shows us Jesus' divine nature most clearly. He has come from the glory and demonstrates, in his life and ministry, that glory for all to see (perhaps the shock is that – just as today- many fail to see it!). Even at his first miracle (or 'sign' as John calls it), the turning of the water into wine, his glory is revealed (John 2:11). Yet we also see in John's gospel evidence of his humanity: he attends a wedding (John 2), presumably socialising and enjoying the occasion as any man might; he gets tired (John 4:6); later weeping with Mary (John 11:35); blood and water flow from his side when he is pierced by a spear at his death (John 19:34).

Fully Man

For this reason he had to be made like his brothers in every way...
(Hebrews 2:17)

So far perhaps, despite these references to his creatureliness, if John's gospel was all we had to go on, it still might be unclear how real Jesus' humanity was and to what degree he truly became flesh. The verse above from Hebrews however challenges any sense that it was a humanity any less than our own. The writer makes the astonishing statement that Jesus was made like us '...in every way'. Jesus was limited in his humanity just as we are! He too had limits to his physical strength and endurance, he too had an intellectual capacity beyond which he could not stretch, and he had emotions— just as we do.

Like Hebrews, the synoptic gospels (Matthew, Mark and Luke) also understand Jesus as a real man. For example, one of Luke's central themes in his gospel and in Acts of the Apostles is the power which comes from the Holy Spirit and the Spirit's ongoing ministry through the life of the early church. At Pentecost (Acts 2) the Holy Spirit transformed the apostles from well-intentioned but ultimately fearful and impotent disciples into effective witnesses, but even before that, the Holy Spirit was at work in the life and ministry of Jesus.

Jesus was conceived by the Holy Spirit (Luke 1:35; cf. Matthew 1:20), and received power to enable his ministry when the Holy Spirit descended upon him at his baptism (Luke 3:22). He needed the Holy Spirit to fulfil his ministry which began at this point (he had performed no miracles before now). If Jesus needed the Holy Spirit, he must have been limited in some way without the Holy Spirit, and the limits were that he was truly a man. The Holy Spirit is important in Luke's account because so is Jesus' humanity or, to put it the other way around, Jesus' humanity is important for Luke because the power that comes from baptism in the Holy Spirit is the main point of Luke and Acts.

After his baptism Jesus faces a very real test as '…the Spirit sent him out into the desert' (Mark 1:12), and 'Jesus, full of the Holy Spirit returned from the Jordan and was led by the Spirit into the desert' (Luke 4:1). In the desert he is tempted and forty days later, in both gospel accounts, his ministry begins. At the conclusion of the testing in the desert 'Jesus returns to Galilee *in the power of the Spirit…* (Luke 4:14)'. The power from on high – the Holy Spirit - explains Jesus' miracles, not any innate divine nature he owns.

It is even the Holy Spirit who was the source of the joy Jesus expressed when his disciples returned from their mission, themselves full of joy at the results they had seen: 'At that time, Jesus, full of joy *through the Holy Spirit…*' (Luke 10:21).

Jesus' Ministry Begins

In the power of the Spirit, Jesus then taught in the synagogues around Nazareth, where he had been brought up. When he stood up to read in the Synagogue at Nazareth itself, Jesus was handed the scroll of Isaiah and he himself unrolled it to the place where the prophet had spoken, centuries before, of the servant of the Lord who, would one day, be an agent by which God would restore Israel:

> *'The Spirit of the Lord is upon me, because he has anointed me to preach good news to the poor. He has sent me to proclaim freedom for the prisoners, and recovery of sight for the blind, to release the oppressed, to proclaim the year of the Lord's favour'. Then he rolled up the scroll, gave it back to the attendant and sat down. The eyes of everyone in the Synagogue were fastened on him, and he began by saying to them, 'Today this scripture is fulfilled in your hearing'.*
> (Luke 4:18-21)

Jesus identifies himself as the one Isaiah spoke of as he saw ahead through the centuries (Isaiah 61), and in doing so lays out his ministry manifesto. It is the Spirit of the Lord who is upon him enabling him to fulfil Isaiah's prophecy.

Jesus' Prayer Life

The Sovereign LORD has given me an instructed tongue, to know the word that sustains the weary. He wakens me morning by morning, wakens my ear to listen like one being taught.
(Isaiah 50:4)

Very early in the morning, while it was still dark, Jesus got up, left the house, and went off to a solitary place, where he prayed.
(Mark 1:35)

Mark describes Jesus going off to pray alone, after a busy time the previous evening healing the sick at Capernaum (Mark 1:29-34). Here Jesus again fulfils what Isaiah spoke of, he rises early to go and spend time with his Father. His need to do this is even more clearly shown in Luke where Jesus spent all night praying before choosing his disciples:

One of those days Jesus went out to a mountainside to pray, and spent the night praying to God. When morning came, he called his disciples to him and chose twelve of them . . .
(Luke 6:12-13)

Why would he have needed to do that if he operated with a divine nature that he 'turned on' when he wanted to be free of his human restrictions and 'be God'? No—Jesus certainly had the most intimate relationship with his Father in heaven, and he needed to nurture this relationship and seek his Father in prayer just as we do. According to the New Testament writers, his lifestyle was one of rising early and seeking God on his own. Luke tells us later, '...he often withdrew to lonely places and prayed.' (5:16)

In Hebrews we read how he prayed, and it is uncomfortable reading for any who insist on a quiet prayer life! 'During the days of Jesus' life on earth, he offered up prayers and petitions with loud cries and tears to the one who could save him from death, and he was heard because of his reverent submission.' (5:7) No wonder he withdrew to lonely places to pray—he prayed with passion, not as one who shared the privileged position of being divine with the Father, but more as one who was walking in fullness of humanity, crying out to him in sure knowledge of his need of God to fulfil what he was called to do. For Jesus this meant to stand against every temptation to turn away from the continual challenge of choosing to walk in righteousness, and to eventually follow his Father's will obediently to the cross.

Jesus' Ministry: Galilee then Jerusalem

According to the synoptic Gospels Jesus spent the major part of his ministry in the region of Galilee. Away from Jerusalem (though not completely hidden from the religious authorities who from time to time came up to see for themselves what he was doing) he pursued what was, on the face of it, a successful ministry. Crowds, in the main, loved him and followed him everywhere enjoying the revival scenes as many were healed, delivered and set free by his miracles and teaching. He taught 'as one with authority, not like the teachers of the law'. (Mark 1:22) During these three years or so he trained his disciples (who apparently remained remarkably dim and untrained, constantly misunderstanding what Jesus told them—at least according to Mark), and preached the Kingdom of God, demonstrating it wherever he went.

But then, at Caesarea Philippi, there is a turning point (e.g. Mark 8:27-30). It is here that Peter receives revelation of Jesus' true identity and the focus of his mission now shifts; his Galilean ministry is drawing to a close and the time has come to turn and head towards the final confrontation. Luke tells us: 'As the time approached for him to be taken up to heaven, Jesus resolutely set out for Jerusalem.' (9:51) This language reminds us again of Isaiah's servant figure: 'because the Sovereign LORD helps me, I will not be disgraced. Therefore *I have set my face like flint*, and I know that I will not be put to shame' (50:7). In the verses immediately before these, Isaiah describes the servant offering his cheeks to those who beat him and not hiding his face from mocking and spitting. Jesus turned away from the relative ease of his Galilean ministry, and, knowing what was ahead, set his face like flint for Jerusalem.

In between Peter's revelation and Jesus turning towards Jerusalem (several days journey away from Galilee), Jesus takes Peter, James and John—his closest disciples—up a mountain and is 'transfigured' before them. The account in Luke is particularly interesting as we once again consider his humanity. We read that two men, Moses and Elijah, appeared in splendour with him. Luke tells us 'they spoke about his departure, which he was about to bring to fulfilment at Jerusalem…' (9:31). What on earth did they say—and why Moses and Elijah?

The answer remarkably demonstrates how much Jesus was like us. Walking in faith, acting in sheer obedience to his Father's will, he was to head towards the cross and separation from his relationship with his Father which he had enjoyed for his entire human life. He knew it would lead to his death, he spoke as much to Peter at Caesarea Philippi and several times en route to Jerusalem making it very clear to his disciples what would happen to him there (e.g. Mark 10:33-4, though they still didn't understand). A man, made like his brothers in every way, Jesus needed encouragement as he prepared for his final journey. None of his disciples could provide this so his Father sent Moses and Elijah to stand with him.

In the same way, when we are faced with a 'faith' challenge we need encouragement from one with spiritual discernment and faith—not from one less equipped than we are ourselves. We need to be encouraged to keep going towards our cross, and not to give up! When I was considering whether it really was the right thing to do to give up my well-paid job and position in the world to go to train at Bible College in obedience to the call of God, I struggled to make the final decision that meant a 'burning of the bridges'. If I left, there was no way back to the position I held at that time in the Police service. I went through a hard time of testing before I reached the point where I could say 'yes!' Along the way, I recall, some well-meaning friends in the church I attended urged me to 'be sensible'. That was not what I needed to hear! Suddenly every reason why it was not sensible to pack in my secure career and venture into the unknown came to mind intensifying the struggle (especially as I could anyway have waited only another eleven years to retire at a still relatively young age).

No—I needed someone to come alongside and say to me, 'Trust God! He has called you and he will provide everything—have faith!'

Jesus needed encouragement just as we do. Moses and Elijah were dispatched to provide that encouragement to Jesus in a way that even his three closest disciples weren't able to. Peter had just followed up the revelation of who Jesus was by rebuking him for the suggestion that he would die (Mark 8:32), and Jesus had had to retort 'get behind me Satan!' Peter was certainly in no position to stand with him in faith for what lay ahead.

On the other hand, these two Old Testament prophets had, like Jesus, been called to demonstrate 'signs and wonders' in their ministries, and had had to confront those opposing God's purposes just as Jesus would.

Moses had repeatedly confronted the Egyptian Pharaoh, demonstrating the superiority of the power of God over the Egyptian gods (Exodus 5-11); and Elijah had stood against the prophets of Baal, again demonstrating the pre-eminence of God with great signs and wonders, this time to the priests of the pagan god Baal. In the demonstration of signs and wonders—the in-breaking of the Kingdom of God to a pagan world—confronted by the priests of that world, Jesus' ministry closely resembled theirs. They alone could stand with him and, '...speak about his departure (from this world) which he was about to bring to fulfilment at Jerusalem', encouraging him to set his face like flint towards the Father's will.

The miracle here for me was not that God sent Moses and Elijah, but that Jesus needed encouragement!

So, duly encouraged, he set his face like flint and travelled to Jerusalem, where he confronted the religious authorities who were angered and threatened by the impact he made on the Jews there. They plotted to capture, try and crucify him. His last serious test, at least as far as the biblical accounts go, was in the garden of Gethsemane. It is not that the cross was not a test, of course it was, but it is as though the temptation to pull back from the horror of it all was played out during the time of wrestling in prayer in that garden, and that once the victory was won in prayer, then the outcome of the test on the cross itself was certain.

Jesus Tempted

Jesus, who was 'made like us in every way' knew temptation just as we do. This is great comfort to us! '…For we do not have a High Priest who is unable to sympathise with our weaknesses, but we have one who has been tempted in every way, just as we are—yet was without sin.' (Hebrews 4:15)

Earlier in Hebrews we read that it was God who made Jesus '…perfect through suffering'. (2:10b) How astonishing to consider Jesus as one who had to be made perfect—surely as the Son of God he was already perfect? Yet had Jesus sinned, had he had a condemning attitude, or even a negative thought, towards those who banged the nails into his hands at his crucifixion, for instance, he wouldn't have remained perfect. He wouldn't have been the '…lamb without blemish or defect' (1 Peter 1:19). He didn't become perfect until his work was completed—until he was able to cry, as he did on the cross, 'It is finished!' and arrive at the point of death having resisted, in his humanity, every single temptation that he had faced.

It is not that at any stage of the process that he wasn't perfect, but that it was a process which had to be completed. Theologians may argue about whether Jesus could have sinned, but unless he was capable of falling he could hardly have been tempted just as we are.

When we stand against temptation there is a degree of suffering involved! There's a wrestling which is often uncomfortable. As we seek to resist, it costs us something. Of course there is no suffering when we just give in to temptation, at least in the short term! Jesus spent his whole human existence led by the Spirit, walking in righteousness—choosing at every moment to resist temptation—and suffered accordingly: 'Because he himself suffered when he was tempted, he is able to help those who are being tempted.' (Hebrews 2:18)

In the garden Jesus implores his Father to find another way, to take away the necessity for him to go to the cross. "Father, if you are willing, take this cup from me; yet not my will but yours be done!" (Luke 22:42) The distress and torment of such a moment can only be guessed at. This was no semi-divine figure calmly facing something that couldn't hurt him anyway—no, Jesus as fully man was facing the full dreadfulness of an imminent, painful death and separation from the one whom he intimately knew as his Father in heaven.

An angel from heaven appeared to him and strengthened him. (22:43). As angels had attended him in the desert at the outset of his ministry the first time the devil had tempted him (Mark 1:13), so angels again appear to strengthen him. Interestingly, after the angels came and gave him strength he didn't get up and walk away, now strong, but '…being in anguish prayed more intently, and his sweat was like drops of blood falling to the ground.' (Luke 22:44) The angels didn't do the work for him, but enabled him to pray even more intensely, and from this point onwards he had all he needed to endure what lay ahead.

As with the transfiguration scene, God didn't lift Jesus above his humanity but strengthened him in it. So for us, we are not always rescued from difficult circumstances in our lives, but God always meets us in them, giving us the strength and encouragement to walk his way.

To continue the story of my own wrestling in response to God's call: when I finally came to the point of saying 'yes' to God it wasn't that somehow by heaving myself above the fears and uncertainties I managed to set my face like flint towards Sussex. What actually happened was that, as I knelt, slumped, by my bed one evening - torn in two by the choice in front of me, I sensed Jesus at my side reminding me of his wrestling at Gethsemane. I can't quite recall now whether this enabled me to pray more earnestly, but I do remember the encounter with the Lord lifting me high above all the self concern and anxiety and enabling me to say 'yes!' Not reluctantly or grudgingly, but with great peace and joy. Interestingly, the things I was wrestling with during that time have never become an issue in the eight years since, in other words, the things I imagined would be difficult weren't once I stepped out – and for that I give God all the glory and thank him for his wonderful grace.

Jesus had the highest call of any man who has ever walked this earth. He experienced intimate relationship with his Father in heaven and out of this relationship lived in constant revelation of the awesomeness of God. Walking in such revelation meant that any cost was worth paying, though in setting his face like flint towards the cross there still remained genuine temptations to overcome. It wasn't because he was God that he walked in this way, but in a true humanity empowered and informed by the Spirit. For the joy set before him—that which God had shown him—he endured the cross (see Hebrews 12:2).

If the battle was mainly won in the garden of Gethsemane the full horror of the cross still lay ahead. Abandoned by his disciples Jesus now suffers the agony of rejection by almost all and of course, most painfully, by his Father in heaven. In Mark's account the sense of rejection and abandonment is the most vivid. Having been mocked by the soldiers who 'enthroned' him (ironically failing to recognise the king of kings!) by placing a purple robe and crown of thorns on his head, they then spat on him, and struck him on the head with a stick (Mark 15:17-20). On the cross three separate groups of people turn against him: firstly, 'those who passed by hurled insults at him' (15:29); the ones who had cried 'Hosanna' a week earlier now derided him; secondly, the '…Chief Priests and teachers of the law mocked him among themselves…' (v.31) and finally even his fellow victims joined in: 'Those crucified with him also heaped insults on him.' (v.32) A small number of women who loved him were there, but even they stood at a distance (v.40).

At the point of death, at midday, darkness came over the whole land, fulfilling the ancient words of Amos: 'On that day...I will make the sun go down at noon and darken the whole earth in broad daylight' (Amos 8:9) and Jesus cries out the most agonising cry of all: 'My God, my God, why have you forsaken me?' Some say that he meant to refer to the whole of Psalm 22, of which these are the opening words, but such a notion undermines and detracts from the full awfulness of the scene. How could he theologise at such a moment? Having been deserted and betrayed by all, taunted and mocked by fellow criminals, ridiculed by Israel's religious leaders, he now experiences complete desolation as even God forsakes him. Here he identifies with our human condition absolutely.

Conclusion

God left eternity and truly became flesh, one of those he had made. He never denied or suppressed his humanity and neither must we. He was fully man and fully God. He knew what it was to be really human; indeed he was the perfect expression of what it means to be human in a world of otherwise inauthentic expressions. He showed us how we might live—how we were originally intended to live—in intimate communion with our maker, proclaiming and demonstrating God's Kingdom, loving our fellow man and subduing the rest of creation.

At the beginning of Jesus' ministry John the Baptist saw that he came from heaven to live perfectly and die a sacrificial death: 'Behold the Lamb of God, who takes away the sin of the world!' (John 1:29) Pilate, without comprehending the profundity of what he was saying, spoke with similar accuracy at the end of Jesus' ministry, when, as the High Priests were preparing the Passover lambs for slaughter in the outer rooms of the Temple, he declared: 'Behold the man!' (John 19:5b)

PART TWO

Study Guide

These notes consist of three sets of questions, which, I suggest, can be used over three consecutive meetings. They are ideal to use in a church house-group or existing The Way of the Spirit group. Not every question has an answer that can be found in the text (although most can). All questions are designed to stimulate further thought and discussion. Be careful not to get distracted by fruitless theological intricacies or argument! The questions should not require lengthy answers.

1. First, read the part of the booklet as specified each week. Look up and read the Biblical passages referred to.

2. Second, read the passages at the head of the questions (if different). Now referring back to the booklet as required, answer all the questions.

3. Write down your answers, as briefly as possible, using only a few words, or at most a couple of sentences each time. As you do so, pray the Lord will show you how your reading and answers are to relate to your own life as a Christian.

4. If you discuss the readings in a group, try to keep to the set themes. It is so easy to go off at tangents, consider many interesting topics and, in the end, miss the whole purpose of the study. The questions are to help you avoid doing that, by keeping your thoughts focussed on the important, central issues.

5. If you use the CD that goes with this booklet, listen to it straight through in one sitting before you start your study; then listen to it again in parts relating to the study you are doing at the time. It contains one continuous sermon.

6. In a group, do not hurry the study. Its purpose is to help you grow spiritually as well as in understanding, and that takes prayer as well as reading.

Week One (pages 10-14)

Mark 4:35 – 5:20

Is it man or God stilling the storm and working the miracle of deliverance here?

Fully man inspired by HS

To what extent have you seen Jesus as truly human in your Christian walk?

full range of human emotions (wept, agony in temple moneychangers, asleep on cushion, withdraws to mountain.

John 1:1-18

In your own words, what is John saying here about where Jesus has come from?

Came from the Father, full of grace and truth

'The Word became flesh and made his dwelling among us.' (v. 14a) It has always been God's desire and purpose to dwell among his people. Where in the Old Testament do we see this purpose expressed?

David in Ark of covenant ✓ in the tabernacle
✓ Before his people as exited Egypt

A Study of Jesus' Humanity

How has Jesus made the Father known (v. 18)?

Through being him ✓
through his life, actions, bringing healing, wholeness etc — see Isaiah 61

Hebrews 2:10-18

What does it mean that Jesus was made 'perfect through suffering' (v. 10; also see v. 18)?

- *Grew into fullness of himself thro' suffering. Nor adult perfection removed from us but accepting that issue of suffering and unite from it*

How easy is it for you to resist temptation? How do you do it?

- *Intimacy of relationship with God*
- *Access to HS*
- *beware of moral high ground*
- *move into muddy waters / grey areas*

What does v. 17 tell us about Jesus' humanity whilst on earth? How did it compare with our own human condition?

- *He became like us 'in every way'.*
- *In order that he might become a merciful & faithful high priest interceding to God*

Week Two (Pages 14-16)

Luke 3:21-23; 4:1-21

What do these passages tell us about the way the Holy Spirit related to Jesus?

Why does Jesus quote this passage from Isaiah (Luke 4:18-19)? In what way might this passage be a 'manifesto' for his ministry?

Why do you need power from the Holy Spirit?

Mark 1:35; Luke 5:16, 6:12-16; Hebrews 5:7

What do these passages teach you about Jesus' prayer life? How does it compare with your own?

Why did Jesus, the Son of God, need to pray so much? Why do you?

Review

What have you learned about Jesus' humanity so far during this study?

A Study of Jesus' Humanity

Week Three (pages 16-22)

Mark 1

Jesus taught as one with authority, not as the teachers of the law. Where did this authority come from?

What different responses can you find from people in this chapter towards Jesus?

Why did Jesus' teaching provoke these responses? Why was his teaching different from that of the Pharisees and teachers of the law?

Luke 9

Why did Moses and Elijah appear to Jesus, and what did they talk to him about? (v. 30-31)

Who do you go to when you need encouraging in the things of God and why?

What motivated Jesus to resolutely set out for Jerusalem? When we walk in faith it has to be faith in God's word to us. What word from God was Jesus holding on to?

Luke 22

What is the evidence of Jesus' humanity in this scene? What was God's response to his prayers?

Jesus, the man, turned and looked straight at Peter (v.61). How do you think Peter felt? How would Peter have responded to the servant girl after Pentecost?

Mark 15

How often in this chapter is Jesus mocked for being a 'King'? Pilate almost seemed to see who Jesus really was—why did he give in to the crowd?

How did the four different groups of people respond to him on the cross?

A Study of Jesus' Humanity

How did Jesus remain sinless in the face of such cruelty from his fellow men?

Review

What revelation of Jesus' humanity have you had during these three weeks?

How has it changed your perception of God?

What implications are there for your own Christian walk?

J² God's descendant. His DNA was human (Mary) and divine (Holy Spirit). So he is different to us whose DNA is human (mother and father). In so far as he is human he is like us but ...

The Way of the Spirit
Home and Further Study Courses

The Way of the Spirit is a series of Bible reading and study programmes, giving a guide to the whole Bible as seen through the activity and experience of the Holy Spirit.

Six levels of study and training are available:

1. Short Bible Reading Courses
• 4-6 weeks • on certain Biblical themes • for home or group study.

2. The full length Bible Reading Course
• 4 six-month parts • giving complete coverage of the Bible • for home, correspondence, group, church, or college use.

3. Biblical Commentaries
• 8 weeks • more detailed studies of single books of the Bible • for home or group study.

4. Biblical and Prophetic Faith (Certificate)
• Two years • the full Bible course plus discipleship and ministry training • local group, class and seminar teaching.

5. Prophetic Bible Teaching (Diploma)
• One year • Part time training for local church or group Bible teaching • three short residential schools and monitored home study

6. Prophetic Bible Teaching (full-time training)
• Variable duration depending on qualifications and experience • a course for training Bible teachers for more long-term works • full-time residential training.

For details of any of these courses, please write to:
The Way of the Spirit, Unit 6, 2b High Street,
Loddon, Norfolk NR14 6AH
Or visit our web site **http://www.thewayofthespirit.com**